ADVENT
Alphabet

RAY PRITCHARD

Table of Contents

Advent from A to Z...1

December 1: Angels 3

December 2: Bethlehem 5

December 3: Circumcised 7

December 4: Dwelt 9

December 5: East 11

December 6: Fullness 13

December 7: Glory 15

December 8: Hope 17

December 9: Inn 19

December 10: Just 21

December 11: Kingdom 23

December 12: Leaped 25

December 13: Manger 27

December 14: Night 29

December 15: Opposed 31

December 16: Ponder 33

December 17: Question 35

December 18: Remember 37

December 19: Sign 39

December 20: Terrified 41

December 21: Until 43

December 22: Virgin 45

December 23: Wonder 47

December 24: X 49

December 25: You 51

December 26: Zion 53

This Advent devotional guide comes from
Keep Believing Ministries.

You can find us on the Internet at
www.KeepBelieving.com.

Questions or Comments?
Email: *ray@keepbelieving.com*

Advent from A to Z

HAVE YOU EVER TRIED to explain the real meaning of Christmas to a child? It isn't easy. There is so much tradition mixed up with spiritual truth that it's sometimes hard to tell Jesus from Santa Claus and the Wise Men from the snowmen.

Sometimes our children have a hard time understanding what it all means. The first frame of a newspaper cartoon shows a mother reading the Christmas story to her young son. The lad has a puzzled look on his face as he sorts it all out. Then he thinks to himself, "Let me see if I've got this straight … Christmas is baby Jesus' birthday, but I get the presents?" The final frame shows him with a satisfied grin as he says to himself, "Is this a great religion or what?!"

I suppose that's how a lot of people think about Christmas.

When our oldest son had just turned two, we bought him the "Christmas ABC Book." We kept it for many years until the binding fell apart. Each letter of the alphabet connects with the biblical story in a little rhyme. For instance,

A means Angel … An Angel was the first to tell
That Christ had come on earth to dwell.

D means Donkey … A Donkey followed Joseph's track
And carried Mary on his back.

(That's okay, even though the Bible doesn't mention a donkey. Mary might have ridden a donkey since she was in the late stages of her pregnancy.)

It's good for all of us to see through the tinsel and fantasy to the great story of Bethlehem.

That's what we're going to do during this Advent journey. Each letter of the alphabet teaches us something important about the Christmas story. Along the way we'll meet the Wise Men, the shepherds, and a bad king named Herod. We'll also meet Joseph and Mary. Best of all, we'll meet the One whose birthday we celebrate.

Our Advent Alphabet begins on December 1. Each devotional ends with a prayer, a QR code, and a link to a YouTube video of a Christmas song. To use the QR code, open your smartphone's camera app and point the camera at the code. Then tap on the link that appears to go straight to the YouTube video page. I hope you'll take time to read the prayer out loud and then watch the video. Those two things will point your heart in the right direction.

I invite you to journey with us through the Advent Alphabet as we prepare for the coming of Christ. If you're ready, let's start with the letter A ...

December 1

Angels

"Suddenly there was with the angel a multitude of the heavenly host praising God"

— Luke 2:13

Have you ever seen an angel?

For most of us, the answer is no. Angels are usually invisible. But now and then God pulls back the curtain and lets us see what is going on in heaven.

That's what happened one night long ago in the fields around Bethlehem.

Suddenly the angels showed up!

If we had been there, would we have seen them? Could the sound of their voices be heard in other places, or did the angels reveal themselves only to the shepherds? We cannot fully answer these questions, but this much is certain: The angels were really there, and the shepherds really did hear them.

It is impossible to miss the supernatural element in the birth of Jesus. Angels pop up all over the Christmas story. An angel tells Mary she will give birth to Jesus. An angel tells Joseph not to worry but to take Mary as his wife. An angel warns Mary and Joseph to flee to Egypt. An angel tells them when it's safe to return to Israel. An angel announces the birth of Christ to the shepherds, and then the angelic choir serenades them.

But that's not all. You have the mysterious star that led the Wise Men from some distant land all the way to Bethlehem to the very house where they found the baby Jesus. The Wise Men were warned not to return to Herod but to go home another way in a dream. So there you have it—angels and stars and dreams. Supernatural stuff everywhere.

We believe something amazing.

Many miracles surround Christmas—the angels, the star, the dreams, the prophecies, and most of all, the virgin birth. They are signs from heaven that we have been visited by Someone from the "other world."

Someone from the world of light came to the world of darkness.

Someone from the eternal came to the temporary.

Someone from heaven came to live with us on earth.

It is right at this point that Christmas becomes so important to us. *We are a dying race living on a dying planet.* All that we see around us will someday vanish without a trace. Despite our best efforts, there is nothing we can do to save ourselves. If we are to be saved, salvation must come from somewhere else. That's the true meaning of Christmas.

The angels bring good news of great joy, the best news the world has ever heard. There are more miracles to come.

Our Father, as we begin this Advent journey, open our hearts so that we might believe in Jesus all over again. Amen.

Musical Bonus
Let's start the music of Advent with an acoustic version of *O Come, All Ye Faithful*
by Lincoln Brewster.
https://youtu.be/WNI8FWKFheE

December 2

Bethlehem

"Joseph also went up from Galilee, from the town of Nazareth, to Judea, to the city of David, which is called Bethlehem, because he was of the house and lineage of David"

— Luke 2:4

"O LITTLE TOWN OF BETHLEHEM, how still we see thee lie."

It's a perfect description.

A more out-of-the-way town could hardly be found in Judea. Bethlehem had only one claim to fame. A thousand years earlier David had been born there. He had been a shepherd on the hills outside the village. If there had been a Chamber of Commerce, they would have put up a billboard: "Welcome to Bethlehem—Home of King David." But they didn't have to do that because all the Jews knew a prophet named Micah had predicted the Messiah would one day be born in Bethlehem (Micah 5:2).

It's not a likely place for the birth of the Son of God.

We would probably choose Rome or Athens.

That would make more sense.

But God chose an out-of-the-way village in a forgotten corner of the Roman Empire.

That's where it all started.

Somewhere I ran across this statement: *God declared war at Bethlehem.*

That's hardly the way we think of it, but it is not unbiblical. Ever since Eden, a battle has been raging between God and Satan for control of planet earth. When Adam and Eve sinned, Satan struck a blow for evil. All the pain and suffering we see around us–every bit of it–can be traced back to that fateful moment in the Garden of Eden. Since then, the armies of evil have been on the march in every generation.

5

They have landed wave after wave of soldiers on beachheads around the world. There are times when it seems as if the battle is over and evil will reign forever.

But if Christmas means anything, it is this: *God wins in the end.* At Bethlehem he launched a mighty counteroffensive that continues to this very day. It started with a tiny baby boy named Jesus, born in a scandalous way, in a barn, to teenagers who were homeless and alone. The world had no idea what God was up to. Only in retrospect do we understand.

The familiar words of Phillips Brooks are a delight at this point:

> How silently, how silently, the wondrous gift is given.
> So God imparts to human hearts the blessings of his heaven.
> No ear may hear his coming but in this world of sin,
> Where meek souls will receive him still, the dear enters in.

So he does! May that be your experience this Christmas season.

My God, you choose the weak things of the world to confound the mighty. Teach me to trust you and not in my own strength or wisdom. Help me to live for your glory alone. Amen.

Musical Bonus
After visiting the Holy Land in 1865, Pastor Phillips Brooks wrote a poem about Christmas Eve in Bethlehem. Several years later, his organist composed a tune to go with the poem. Let's listen as BeBe Winans sings a soulful arrangement of *O Little Town of Bethlehem*. https://youtu.be/Iunf84Bp1-Y

Circumcised

"At the end of eight days, when he was circumcised, he was called Jesus, the name given by the angel before he was conceived in the womb"

— Luke 2:21

THIS MAY BE THE MOST forgotten verse in the Christmas story. But there is something here we need to notice.

The baby was circumcised and officially given the name Jesus on the eighth day after his birth.

What would it cost Jesus to provide for our salvation? He paid for our sins with the price of his own blood. Here is the vital connection. Jesus is just one week old, and already he enters into the pain of human existence. *Eight days old and his blood is already being shed.*

Joseph probably performed the circumcision himself. If that is true, then it is also symbolic. Jesus begins his life by shedding his own blood at the hand of his Father. Those few drops of blood point to the bloody way his life will end. The infant's cradle is tinged with a crimson reflection from the Redeemer's cross.

A Christmas play asks the question, "What did Joseph do the day after Christ was born?" We assume he helped with Mary and the baby, making things as comfortable as he could. But what about the next day? The play imagines that since Joseph is a carpenter, he begins making a crib for Jesus. As he does, he recalls the celebration they had with the shepherds and says to himself, "If they treated Him like this when He was just a baby, how will they treat him when they find out he is the Son of God?" At that exact moment in the play, the lights suddenly go off, and all you can hear is a hammer hitting wood as a spotlight splashes its beams on a bloody cross.

A contemporary Christmas card captures this well. A baby's footprint appears on the cover with the words, "Unto you is born this day a Savior." When you open the card, the phrase, "Which is Christ the Lord," is superimposed over a grown man's handprint, complete with a bloody hole in the palm.

There is a direct line from his birth to his circumcision to the cross. Circumcision foreshadows the blood he will shed for the sins of the world.

How far is God willing to go? We can't even imagine the answer to that question. There is no pit so deep that the love of God is not deeper still. At Christmastime, we do not celebrate the birth of some aloof God who stands afar off. No, we celebrate the birth of Immanuel— God with us.

How far is God willing to go? Whatever pit you're in, God is willing to enter that pit and meet you there. That's what he did 2000 years ago.

Almighty God, you did not spare yourself from anything. You came all the way to the bottom because that's where we were. Thank you for Jesus Christ, whose blood has set us free. Amen.

Musical Bonus
Dating back to the 8ᵗʰ century, *O Come, O Come, Emmanuel* may be our oldest Christmas carol. Let's enjoy this beautiful version by aeseaes.
https://youtu.be/nMn4TpA0GV0

Dwelt

"The Word became flesh, and dwelt among us"
— John 1:14 NASB

"DWELT" IS AN UNUSUAL WORD.
It means to live among.
One version uses the phrase "moved into the neighborhood."
Everything starts with this fact—that Christ was in the world. He left heaven for a remote village in a forgotten province, to join a despised race, to be born of an obscure teenage peasant girl in a stable, wrapped in rags, placed in a feeding trough instead of a crib.
He was one of us and walked among us.
God himself came down and entered the human race. He moved into the neighborhood and became just like us so that we would hear him saying, "I love you."
Theologians use a particular word to talk about this. *They call the birth of Christ the "Incarnation."* That word means God came to earth and shared our humanity.
The infinite became finite.
The immortal became mortal.
The Creator became the created.
The omnipotent lived inside a young girl's womb.
The Almighty became a helpless baby.
The Deity was wrapped in rags.
The King of the Universe was born in a stable.
As Martin Luther put it, "He whom the worlds could not enwrap yonder lies in Mary's lap."
Read the New Testament again. Instead of flash and splash, there is a frightened father, an exhausted mother, a dirty stable in wintertime, rags for diapers, and a feeding trough. There he is, ignored by the world—a tiny, helpless baby. Immanuel—God with us.

It's so simple you know it must be true. *Only God would have done it that way.*

A young man sat in my office and listened as I explained the gospel to him. Finally he said, "I just can't believe all that stuff." So I asked him, "What would it take for you to believe?" "I would believe if God came down and stood in front of me and told me himself," he said. "My friend, he already has come down," I replied. "He came down 2,000 years ago and lived among us. If you don't believe that, then I have nothing better to offer you."

One of the verses of a famous Christmas carol says it very well:

> Veiled in flesh the God-head see; hail the incarnate Deity.
> Pleased as man with men to dwell, Jesus, our Emmanuel.
> Hark, the herald angels sing, "Glory to the newborn King."

Jesus moved into our neighborhood. Have you met your new neighbor yet?

Lord Jesus, we are glad you moved into our neighborhood. If you had stayed in heaven, we would never have met you. Thank you for making us part of your forever family. Amen.

Musical Bonus
Christmas must become personal for each of us. Let's listen as Sovereign Grace Music sings *Prepare Him Room.*
https://youtu.be/egjsEQ6zKpA

December 5

East

"After Jesus was born in Bethlehem in Judea, during the time of King Herod, Magi from the east came to Jerusalem and asked, 'Where is the one who has been born king of the Jews?'"

— Matthew 2:1-2

A GREAT MYSTERY surrounds the Magi.

Who are they?

Where do they come from?

The term "Magi" refers to a special class of priests in the Persian Empire. We know from other sources that the Magi had existed for hundreds of years before the time of Christ. They had their own religion, their own priesthood, and their own writings. It appears from the book of Daniel that they existed in his day, and it seems Daniel was appointed head over the cast of the Magi in the time of King Nebuchadnezzar (Daniel 5:11).

Who were they? They were the professors and philosophers of their day. They were brilliant and highly educated scholars trained in medicine, history, religion, prophecy and astronomy. They were also trained in what we would call astrology.

These influential leaders served as advisors to the king. It would not be wrong to call them king-makers because they functioned as political advisors to the Persian rulers.

Finally, they were highly-educated men who thought deeply about life, and consequently, it is perfectly legitimate to call them "Wise Men."

We know the Jews and Persians had intermingled for at least 500 years. *It seems that they considered Daniel (who was Jewish) as one of their own.* Since the time of Daniel, the Persians had known of the Jewish expectation of a Messiah. It is possible that they even knew from the prophecy of the "70 weeks" in Daniel 9 the approximate time of his coming. What they did not know was the exact time. When they saw the star, they knew the time had come.

Think of how many barriers they had to cross to get to Jesus. There was a culture barrier, a distance barrier, a language barrier, a racial barrier, a religious barrier, not to speak of a hostile king and indifferent religious leaders. It wasn't easy for them to find Jesus, but they did.

If they found him, then so can you.

Lord Jesus, grant us the zeal of the Wise Men first to find you and then to tell others where they can find you too. Amen.

Musical Bonus
Most versions of *We Three Kings* tend to be on the somber side. Here's a lilting version of *We Three Kings* by Blackmore's Night. https://youtu.be/YnvZ37wTrWA

Fullness

"But when the fullness of time had come, God sent forth his Son"

— Galatians 4:4

THE WORD "FULLNESS" SPEAKS of something complete and fully developed, like a ripe apple ready to be picked or like a pregnant woman feeling labor pains, ready to deliver her baby. It describes the moment in history when the stage was perfectly set. At that moment, not earlier and not later, God sent forth his Son.

Think of how unlikely it all seems:

A decree from Caesar Augustus.
An angel appears to Mary.
A virgin becomes pregnant.
An angel comes to Joseph in a dream.
A baby called Immanuel.
A mysterious star in the east.
Wise Men showing up in Jerusalem.
Angels appearing to shepherds.
A trip to Bethlehem.
No room in the inn.
A stable that was available.
A babe wrapped in rags and placed in a feeding trough.
A star that led the Wise Men to the right house in Bethlehem.
Gifts of gold, frankincense, and myrrh.
A dying king who tried to kill the baby.
A desperate journey to Egypt.
Another journey to Nazareth.

None of it happened by chance. A pagan emperor issued a decree at just the right moment in history, when the *Pax Romana* was in full force and the world was yearning restlessly for deliverance. Angels showed up to a young man and a young woman who believed what they said. When the virgin became pregnant, Joseph decided not to divorce her. A star began to shine in the east that led the Wise Men to travel hundreds of miles seeking the baby. All of it finally focused on a stable outside an inn in the "little town of Bethlehem," where the most incredible event in history took place.

C. S. Lewis says it this way:

> The central miracle asserted by Christians is the Incarnation. They say that God became Man. Every other miracle prepares the way for this, or results from this.

Sometimes we focus on peripheral questions (how did Jesus turn water into wine?) that distract us from the central truth of our faith. *We believe God became a man.*

The Creator became part of the creation.

The infinite became finite.

Almighty God took on the form of a man and was born as a tiny baby.

This *is* the central truth of our faith.

When everything was just right, God sent his Son to be our Savior.

That's what Christmas is all about.

Lord, thank you for arranging all the details centuries in advance. You set the stage, then Christ was born. Open our eyes so that we may see him clearly. Amen.

Musical Bonus
How about a little reggae Christmas music? If you need an extra dose of joy today, check out *Joy to the World* by Christafari.
https://youtu.be/hyZaJykkIg0

December 7

Glory

"Glory to God in the highest and on earth peace, goodwill toward men"

— Luke 2:14

How many times have we heard those words?

How many times have we seen them printed on Christmas cards?

How many times have we repeated them?

These words contain three promises that are directly connected with the coming of Christ to the earth:

1. *Glory* to God in the Highest.
2. Peace on Earth.
3. Goodwill Toward Men.

Unfortunately, it's hard to find "peace on earth" and "goodwill among men" nowadays. If you want to know what's wrong with the world, look in the mirror. The problem is you, the problem is me, the problem is all of us together.

There is no peace on earth because we are not peace-loving people. *We are filled with anger, hate, lust, and greed.*

We were made for glory, but our glory faded a long time ago. First, we disobeyed, then we died on the inside, then we started dying on the outside, then we turned to our own devices, then we said, "God, we don't need you at all. Leave us alone!" And we wonder why the world is the way it is. Look in the mirror. "We have met the enemy, and he is us."

Is there such a thing as peace on earth? The answer is Yes. But the peace Jesus brings is not won around a conference table or at the point of a bayonet. His peace goes from heart to heart to heart.

The angels' message is true. There is such a thing as peace on earth and goodwill toward men. It comes when Jesus Christ comes into a life.

Is it possible to have his peace at Christmastime? Yes, it is.

When Jesus enters your life, he will remove the hatred and bitterness, and he will redeem the hurts of the past.

My prayer for you at Christmastime is that you might experience the peace that Jesus brings.

The glory of God shines forth from that manger in Bethlehem.

His glory still shines today.

One day his glory will fill the earth.

Holy Lord, come and fill us because we are empty without you. Shine through us and fill this dark world with your glory. Amen

Musical Bonus

This familiar carol started in France, made its way to England, and eventually spread around the world. Let's listen to
The First Noel by Stars Go Dim.
https://youtu.be/hB6XvYlRhqU

December 8

Hope

"We have this hope as an anchor for the soul, sure and strong"

— Hebrews 6:19

WHAT DOES THIS VERSE have to do with Christmas?

At first glance, the answer appears to be nothing.

But this verse has everything to do with a promise God made to Abraham four thousand years ago. God promised to give him a land of his own, and he promised him a nation of descendants. He also promised that through Abraham all the nations of the earth would be blessed (Genesis 12:1-3). From this stupendous promise came the nation of Israel and (2000 years later) the Lord Jesus Christ, who is the ultimate "seed of Abraham."

Look at the first verse of the New Testament:

> The book of the genealogy of Jesus Christ, the Son of David, the Son of Abraham — *Matthew 1:1*

Starting with a genealogy doesn't sound very hopeful. After all, Matthew 1 contains all those "begats" we like to skip over because the names are unfamiliar and hard to pronounce.

But that's a mistake.

If you study the list, you soon discover that it reads like a rogue's gallery.

- There is Abraham who lied about his wife (twice!)
- Isaac who lied about Rebekah
- Jacob who was a congenital cheater
- Judah who slept with his daughter-in-law (thinking she was a shrine prostitute)
- David who committed adultery and murder

- Solomon who had hundreds of wives
- and Manasseh, a man whose name is synonymous with evil.

He was so wicked that he sacrificed the children of Judah to the pagan deities.

The list also mentions four women: Tamar slept with Judah, Rahab the harlot, Ruth who was a Moabitess, and Bathsheba who committed adultery with David. Three are Gentiles. Three are involved in some form of sexual immorality. Two are involved in prostitution. One is an adulteress. All four are in the line that leads to Jesus Christ!

In the end, the only name in the genealogy that matters is Jesus. *Everything that happened before was meant to lead to him.* God orchestrated centuries of history to bring his Son to the world at just the right moment.

That's the good news of Christmas.

Is there hope in the world? Yes! *Hope shines from the manger.* If we want that hope to invade our lives, we must come to Bethlehem and bow before the newborn King.

If you have a messed-up past, you can still be part of God's forever family. Reach out to Jesus, and you will find he has already reached out to you.

Father, you are a Promise-keeping God. Thank you for making promises to the undeserving because that includes me. Thank you for everlasting hope that death cannot destroy. Amen.

Musical Bonus
Navigating the Covid-19 pandemic has been difficult for all of us. Matthew West encourages us with *The Hope of Christmas.*
https://youtu.be/x4nF-ktAI54

December 9

Inn

"She brought forth her firstborn son, and wrapped him in swaddling clothes, and laid him in a manger; because there was no room for them in the inn"
— Luke 2:7 KJV

DON'T THINK OF a Holiday Inn.

The "inn" was nothing like that.

It most likely was a guest room in a house in Bethlehem. Perhaps Mary and Joseph went there because they knew the owners. Perhaps they were related. But we all know the result.

No room in the inn.

That's not an incidental detail.

He was born like this so the humble might feel free to come to him. The very manner of his birth—turned away from the inn, born in a stable—means God invites the rejected, the abused, the mistreated, the forgotten, the overlooked, to come to him for salvation. "We might tremble to approach a throne, but we cannot fear to approach a manger" (Charles Spurgeon).

If Jesus had been born in Paris or in Beverly Hills, only the rich and famous would feel at home with him. But since he was born in a stable, all the outsiders of the world (and there are far more outsiders than insiders) instinctively feel a kinship with him.

Is there a hint here of his upcoming death? I believe there is. Turned away from the inn and resting in a feeding trough, he was already bearing the only cross a baby can bear—extreme poverty and the contempt and indifference of mankind.

This baby lying forgotten in an exposed stable, resting in a feeding trough, is God's appointed "sign" to us all. This is a true incarnation. *God has come to the world in a most unlikely way.* This is what Philippians 2:7 means when it says he *"emptied himself, by taking the form of a servant, being born in the likeness of men.* "Nothing about the baby Jesus appeared supernatural. There were no halos, no angels visible, and no choirs singing. If you had been there, you might have concluded this was just a baby born to a young couple down on their luck. Nothing about the outward circumstances pointed to God. Yet all of it—every part of it, every single, solitary, seemingly random detail—was planned by the Father before the foundation of the world. To the unseeing eye, nothing looks less like God; to those who understand, his fingerprints are everywhere.

There was no room for Jesus that night in Bethlehem. Will you make room for him in your heart this year?

My Lord, though the world has no room for you, come and dwell in my heart today. Amen.

Musical Bonus

Here's some good news for a world filled with darkness. Future of Forestry reminds us that *Light Has Come.*
https://youtu.be/8XjSRbc3XjQ

December 10

Just

"Her husband Joseph, being a just man and unwilling
to put her to shame, resolved to divorce her quietly"
— Matthew 1:19

HE'S THE FORGOTTEN MAN of Christmas.

Mary understandably gets more attention.

Yet Joseph is one of the greatest men in the Bible.

Let me briefly list for you the things we know about him:

- His father was Jacob.
- His family hometown was Bethlehem in Judea, but he lived in Nazareth in Galilee. That meant Joseph and Mary had to travel about 95 miles in the dead of winter to register for the census.
- He is from the royal line of David. The genealogy in Matthew 1 makes that clear.
- He was a carpenter by trade.
- He was a poor man. When he and Mary presented Jesus in the temple, they brought a turtledove to sacrifice. Jews only did that when they could not afford a lamb.
- He was a devout man.

Nowhere does his faith shine brighter than when he thinks Mary has been unfaithful to him. *He loved her so much that he was unwilling to expose her to public humiliation.* Instead, he decided to divorce her quietly.

Having made his decision … he didn't do it. As one writer put it, there was a "short but tragic struggle between his legal conscience and his love." Then one night, God spoke to him in a dream.

An angel of the Lord appeared to him in a dream and said, "Joseph, son of David, do not be afraid to take Mary home as your wife, because what is conceived in her is from the Holy Spirit" — *Matthew 1:20*

Joseph needed assurance. He couldn't marry Mary until he was sure it was all right. *He had to know the truth.* God met him at the point of his need at precisely the right moment. He told Joseph the one thing he most wanted to hear: "Joseph, son of David, do not be afraid to take Mary as your wife."

And later, when the angel gave him the good news that the child was conceived through the Holy Spirit, he gladly took her as his wife. He took the baby as his own son and gave him the name Jesus.

In these days of confusion, Joseph shows us what a godly man looks like:

He was strong when he could have been weak.
He was tender when he could have been harsh.
He was thoughtful when he could have been hasty.
He was trusting when he could have doubted.

There is one other line of proof about the kind of man Joseph was. When Jesus grew up and began his ministry, he chose one word above all others to describe what God is like. He called him Father.

Where did he learn about fathers? From Joseph, a good and just man.

Heavenly Father, thank you for choosing Joseph. Grant me that same courage to trust you even when my circumstances make no sense to me. Amen.

Musical Bonus
I ran across the beautiful voices of the choristers from St. George's Chapel, Windsor Castle, in England. For some reason, the video includes footage of the boys playing rugby, which I found fascinating. Let's watch and listen as they sing *Ding Dong Merrily on High*.
https://youtu.be/b3wj0xnBqdg

December 11

Kingdom

"He will reign over the house of Jacob forever, and of his kingdom there will be no end"

— Luke 1:33

IT IS EASY TO FORGET how revolutionary these words must have sounded in the beginning. They were …

Spoken by an angel
To a virgin
Announcing a baby
Who will one day
Rule the world.
And it came totally out of the blue
To a teenage girl who was a virgin
In Nazareth, a minor city in a remote corner of the Roman Empire.
It didn't seem likely.

How would Mary's baby have a kingdom that never ends?

After all, she and Joseph were betrothed (more than engagement, less than what we call marriage), they were poor, she was pregnant, and they didn't have connections with the movers and shakers in ancient Israel.

They were just a young couple facing a crisis pregnancy.

The whole affair would cast a shadow over them and lead to rumors and insinuations that would follow Jesus during his earthly ministry.

Even now, after 2000 years, the angel's message seems mind-blowing.

Jesus has a kingdom.

He is building it in human hearts around the world.

Someday he will return and visibly reign on the earth.

That kingdom—his kingdom—will never end.

There are some men and women who are not like everyone else.

They have been gripped with the thought that the kingdom of God is the greatest thing in the world. That one thought has revolutionized their lives and reoriented their values. Kingdom issues are at stake. That's the only possible explanation for the way they live.

Everyone reading my words has a choice to make. Either you join yourself to the kingdoms of this world that are doomed to fail. Or you join forces with Jesus Christ and follow him as your Savior and Lord.

His kingdom will never end. Why would you follow anyone else?

Lord Jesus, help me to know you, love you, and serve you with joy because you are my one and only King. Amen.

Musical Bonus
We have a special treat today: *God Rest Ye Merry, Gentlemen* by Highlands Worship.
https://youtu.be/OyhTOmOzzb4

December 12

Leaped

"The baby in my womb leaped for joy"
— Luke 1:44

THAT'S WHAT ELIZABETH SAID to Mary when they met.

Elizabeth's baby was John the Baptist.

He evidently started his career early.

We know babies in the womb can see and hear and react to sound and light. Consider a child in his mother's womb in the latter stages of pregnancy. Even before birth, he learns to recognize the voice of his father and mother. Marlene told me that when she was pregnant and sitting in church, each of our three boys recognized my voice from inside the womb and began to move around as soon as I started my sermon. This happened so regularly that it could not have been by chance. They knew my voice in the womb.

It was the same way with John the Baptist.

His whole purpose in life was to point people to Jesus.

He came to prepare the way of the Lord.

He leaped for joy inside his mother's womb, meaning he did a kind of prenatal cartwheel all pregnant mothers understand.

When God filled Elizabeth with the Spirit, her baby leaped within her for joy. Why should this surprise us? The God who can conceive Jesus within Mary's womb can also cause John the Baptist to leap for joy inside Elizabeth's womb. *This miracle would have been a great consolation to Mary in her difficult circumstances.* John was unaware of the meaning of his movement, yet his leaping was inspired by the Lord. The Holy Spirit was at work within him even before he was born.

Does Jesus seem far away to you?

Do you wonder if he really understands?

This passage (Luke 1:39-44) is part of God's answer to you. One writer put it this way:

Two babies meet while still in the womb of their mothers and the Holy Spirit bears witness between them. God comes into the womb of a woman and so identifies with humankind in our weakest, and most vulnerable condition (Presbyterians Pro-Life Monthly, 2009).

This passage shines a light on Christmas because it means our Lord was part of the human race from conception. *He was born on Christmas, but his human life began nine months earlier.* He was truly a Savior who became like us even before he was born.

Consider that the Lord you worship was once an embryo in Mary's womb.

How weak, how frail the Savior appears.

How great a distance the Son must travel to enter our world.

He is truly Immanuel—God with us.

Lord Jesus, may I never take for granted the miracle of your entrance into our world. Amen.

Musical Bonus
Here's a song written to give us hope in troubled times: *Behold Him* by Francesca Battistelli.
https://youtu.be/ulGqyckf-oI

December 13

Manger

"She gave birth to her firstborn son and wrapped him
in swaddling cloths and laid him in a manger"
— Luke 2:7

WHAT'S WRONG WITH this picture?

The answer is simple: *Jesus doesn't belong here.* He's the Son of God from heaven. He doesn't deserve to be treated like a vagrant or a criminal. He deserves the best the world has to offer. He comes from heaven to earth—and ends up in a stable? How can that be? Let me press the point home another way. *God could have done better.* Suppose you had all power and could choose the time, place, and manner of your son's birth. Would you choose to have him born outside, in a stable? That doesn't make any sense.

What's going on here?

The world had no room for Christ then, and it has no room for Christ now. John 1:11 puts it very plainly: *"He came to his own, and his own people did not receive him."* Jesus came "home" to his own people—and they wouldn't take him in. He came to the people who should have known him best, and they wanted nothing to do with him.

If Jesus were born today, it would happen in a ramshackle tenement building, a field in the country, or a remote village in India. The world that had no room for him then has no room for him now.

His humiliation started early and continued to the very end. He was born outside because they wouldn't let Mary and Joseph come inside. During his ministry he told his disciples, *"Foxes have holes and birds of the air have nests, but the Son of Man has no place to lay his head"* (Matthew 8:20).

He owned nothing but the clothes on his back, and when he was crucified, the soldiers gambled for his robe. When he died, they buried him in a borrowed tomb.

He was an "outsider" in every sense—he came from "outside" this earth, he was born "outside" the inn, and he died "outside" the city walls.

The "No Vacancy" signs were there for our benefit. God could have made a room available. He could have created a hospital or a palace in Bethlehem if he had so desired. The sequence of events that unfolded— the census, the long journey, no room at the inn, "no crib for a bed," the feeding trough, the "swaddling clothes"—all of it was planned by God even though it all appeared to happen by chance. God willed there would be no room in the inn not for the sake of Jesus, but for our sakes, that we might learn who Jesus is and why he came.

May God grant to each of us faith to believe and an open heart to say, "Yes, Lord Jesus, there is room in my heart for you."

Lord Jesus, we pray today for those who are struggling to know you. Pull back the curtains of unbelief so that they might be filled with faith to believe in you. Amen.

Musical Bonus
It's time for some country music! Let's listen to *King Size Manger* by Josh Turner.
https://youtu.be/doo3khf1s1w

December 14

Night

"He rose and took the child and his mother by night
and departed to Egypt"

— Matthew 2:14

THE SEQUENCE OF EVENTS goes like this:

1. Joseph and Mary were in Nazareth when the conception of Jesus took place.
2. They traveled to Bethlehem where Jesus was born.
3. Herod the Great ordered all the baby boys under the age of two in Bethlehem to be slaughtered.
4. An angel warned Joseph to take Mary and Jesus and flee to Egypt for safety.
5. They left by night, fled to Egypt, and stayed there until Herod died.
6. Then they returned to Nazareth where Jesus was raised.

There are many mysteries about all this:

1. We don't know how old Jesus was when they went to Egypt.
2. We don't know where they stayed in Egypt.
3. We don't know how long they stayed in Egypt.
4. We don't know how old Jesus was when they returned to Nazareth.

Because Herod wanted the baby Jesus dead, he ordered the male babies of Bethlehem put to death. That's why an angel warned Joseph who took Mary and Jesus during the night and fled to Egypt. After Herod died, an angel told them it was safe to return. But when he heard Herod's son was reigning in his father's place, Joseph took Mary and Jesus and returned to Nazareth.

Matthew 2:14 says Joseph and Mary took Jesus and left during the night, fleeing for Egypt because they feared what Herod might do to their baby. Given Herod's slaughter of the baby boys of Bethlehem, that was a wise move.

Whenever God does anything good in this world, the devil puts his demon spirits into overdrive, stirring up men like Herod to do their dastardly deeds.

The path of life takes many unexpected zigs and zags, and we all find ourselves fleeing to Egypt for safety from time to time. True greatness waits its time. It does not rush the Lord or complain when things happen slowly or when the plans of life suddenly are overturned. By faith we go down to Egypt in the middle of the night, knowing that one day by faith we will come "out of Egypt." Both the going and the coming are part of God's plan for us.

Though he was the Son of God, Jesus had to escape to Egypt in the middle of the night. As he was not exempt from the trials of this world, neither are we. But God will have the last word. Herod will die, Jesus will return home to grow up in safety.

Perhaps you feel as if you are in a dark place at this moment. *Be encouraged, child of God.* Weeping may endure for a night, but joy comes in the morning.

Loving Lord, you ordain both the rising of the sun and the coming of the night. When my way seems dark, light my path so that I might follow you. Amen.

Musical Bonus
It's fun to hear a traditional Christmas carol infused with an Irish lilt. Let's listen as Moya Brennan sings *Angels We Have Heard on High.*
https://youtu.be/-ty9TWXfyd0

December 15

Opposed

"Behold, this child is appointed for the fall and rising of many in Israel, and for a sign that is opposed"
— Luke 2:34

CALL THIS THE BAD NEWS about the good news.

Not everyone loves Jesus.

Not everyone is glad he came.

The scribes ignored him.

Herod tried to kill him.

Their descendants will nail him to a cross.

He is the Great Divider of Men. He will cause many to fall and many to rise. Many will speak against him, and in speaking against him, the hidden thoughts of the heart will be revealed.

What a thing to say about a tiny baby. "Mary, they are going to touch this child, and you won't be able to do anything about it. They are going to hate him, they are going to lie about him, they'll spread rumors about you and Joseph, they will smear his name with malicious lies. You will have to stand by helplessly and watch it happen."

Down the road it all came true. Eventually they questioned not only his parentage, but also his mental ability. They snickered and said, "He thinks he's the Son of God. But he's filled with demons." When hatred took full control, they arrested Jesus and put him on trial as a seditious blasphemer. They beat him within an inch of his life, leaving his skin in tattered ribbons. After the trial, he was condemned to die. In the end, Mary watched her son die an agonizing, brutal, bloody, inhuman death. Amid the stench and gore of crucifixion, Mary stood by her son, unable to staunch the flow of blood, unable to wipe his brow, unable to hold his hand.

It all happened exactly as Simeon had predicted. When Mary watched her son die, a sword pierced her soul. *Above the cradle stands the cross.* This little baby was born to die. Dag Hammarskjold, late Secretary-General of the United Nations, put it this way:

> How proper it is that Christmas should follow Advent. For to him who looks toward the future, the Manger is situated on Golgotha, and the Cross has already been raised in Bethlehem. (*Hymns for the Family of God*, p. 189)

The joy of Christmas leads on to the agony of Good Friday. He was born to end up that way.

Your response to Jesus reveals what is in your heart. But that's not all. Your response to Jesus tells us where you are going and how you are going to get there. But most of all, the way you respond to Jesus tells us where you are going to spend eternity.

Gracious Lord, give me grace to take my stand with Jesus today and never to be ashamed of him. May I have courage to follow Jesus even when the road leads to a cross. Amen.

Musical Bonus

In case you're missing the reason for the season, today's song will bring you back to the heart of Christmas. Let's enjoy *The King is Here* by Love & the Outcome.
https://youtu.be/BIMFLDtkyOk

December 16

Ponder

"Mary treasured up all these things, pondering them
in her heart"

— Luke 2:19

THE WORD "TREASURED" has the idea of counting things up, almost
like making a list so you will not forget anything. It's what you do at
the end of a hectic day, and you want to make sure you don't forget
anything that has happened.

The word "pondered" goes deeper than "wondering." It means to
take the events as you have laid them out in your memory and then
go beneath the surface to understand what it all means and why it
happened the way it did.

No doubt Mary went back to what happened to Zacharias and
Elizabeth and the birth of John the Baptist. I'm sure she thought about
what Gabriel said, how Joseph responded when she told him she was
pregnant, and the amazing dream Joseph had. She must have recalled
the long journey from Nazareth to Bethlehem, and all the events of the
birth itself, including the surprise visit of the shepherds. She certainly
had plenty to think about. No doubt she continued to wonder why
God had chosen her, and I'm sure she pondered what was ahead for
her newborn son.

Pondering is hard work, which is why many of us never get around
to it. *Yet this is the perfect time of year to do it.* What better time than
now to consider what God has been teaching you?

Here is a simple exercise that may help you do some serious
pondering before 2022 arrives:

Set aside at least an hour of uninterrupted time.

Find a quiet place. Turn off the TV and put your smartphone on
silent.

Begin with a prayer asking God to show you the things he wants you to learn.

Then think about the last 12 months. *What has God been teaching you?* What lessons seem to come up again and again? What have you learned about yourself this year?

What have you learned about God's character this year?

Ask the Lord for insight as to where he might be leading you in the year to come.

If you do this exercise with an open heart, God will give you insight about the past and hope for the future.

Mary pondered what God had been doing in her life. Now it's your turn.

My Lord, give me eyes to see your hand at work in my life. When nothing around me makes sense, anchor my heart in you. Amen.

Musical Bonus

I love this hauntingly beautiful arrangement of *Breath of Heaven (Mary's Song)* by Leanna Crawford.
https://youtu.be/XL-mQQ8iauk

Question

"How will this be" Mary asked the angel, "since I am a virgin?"

— Luke 1:34

THIS IS A PERFECTLY natural question.

Mary is betrothed but not formally married. She has never had sexual relations with any man. How then can she become pregnant and bear a son?

Mary does not doubt the angel's word, even though it must have sounded incredible. She believed what the angel said. Her only question had to do with how it would happen.

In essence, she says to Gabriel, "All right. I'm willing to do my part, but you need to explain how we'll handle this one little problem." *That's real faith.* That's believing the impossible. That's trusting God when the "facts" argue against it.

Mary has often been portrayed as a kind of misty, other-worldly figure. If you look at some of the great paintings of Mary, they make her look so peaceful you almost forget she was a real person. That's a shame because Luke makes it clear she was very real, with very real doubts, very real questions, and very real faith.

Nowhere is this seen with more clarity than in verse 38:

"Behold, I am the servant of the Lord; let it be to me according to your word."

Without exaggeration, we may call this one of the greatest statements of faith in all the Bible.

We read it so often that we forget how great it really is. But remember, it's 2:00 in the afternoon, you're 16 years old and very much in love. Your mom asks you to go fetch some water to do the laundry, and on your way to the well, you run into a man you've never seen before. He tells you that you're going to get pregnant, you're going to give birth to a son, and he's going to be the Son of God. When you ask how, he says, "Don't worry about it. The Holy Spirit will cover you like a cloud, and you'll end up pregnant. That's all there is to it." What do you say to that?

Mary said yes. Yes to God, yes to the impossible, yes to God's plan.

When the angel said, "Nothing is impossible with God," Mary took a deep breath and replied, "May everything you said come true." And with those words, Christmas came to the world.

Our Father, we do not pray for more faith. We pray for courage to exercise the faith we already have. Make us like Mary, willing to believe in spite of our doubts. Amen.

Musical Bonus

In 1996 Kenny Rogers and Wynonna Judd recorded a duet that became a fan favorite. Let's listen as they sing *Mary, Did You Know?* https://youtu.be/NGw8holYZr0

Remember

"He has dealt mercifully with our fathers and remembered His holy covenant"

— Luke 1:72

WHAT WAS IT LIKE just before Jesus came to the earth?

Part of the answer comes from the song of Zechariah, father of John the Baptist. You can read the whole song in Luke 1:67-79. Some of it sounds strange to our ears. But that's part of the great value of this passage. *Zechariah's song reveals the deep faith of the Jewish people on the eve of Messiah's birth.* For hundreds of years the people of God had been waiting for Messiah to come. Now at last he is almost here.

All of that is on Zechariah's heart and is comprehended in this one single truth: *At long last God has visited his people!* That means God has kept his promise.

It's hard for us to grasp the magnitude of this thought. *Nobody appeared more forgotten than the Jews chafing under Roman rule.* Reduced to an obscure province in the Roman Empire, they were rejected, overlooked, and despised. Nearly 1,000 years had passed since the glorious days of King David. Over 400 years had passed since their last prophet—a man named Malachi. As Zechariah looks down at his infant son, he knows the crucial moment of world history has arrived. In his arms he holds the baby who will grow up to prepare the way of the Lord. That could only mean one thing:

The Messiah is on the way!

The long wait is over!

God has remembered his promise!

He has visited his people!

Christmas is only one week away. As the commercials keep telling us, there are only 7 shopping days left until Christmas Day. But think about what else that means. There are also …

7 praising days until Christmas
7 singing days until Christmas
7 worshiping days until Christmas

How are you going to spend the 7 days that are left for you before Christmas finally arrives?

Good news, my friend. *Jesus is here at last!* Will you drop everything and welcome him into your heart? Or are you too busy this year to be bothered with him?

Lord Jesus, you remembered me even when I had forgotten you. You came for me when I was running away. Thank you for turning me from an enemy into a friend by your grace. Amen.

Musical bonus

Today's carol was written by William Chatterton Dix in 1865. It became an instant classic. Let's listen as Fernando Ortega sings *What Child is This.*
https://youtu.be/mNyvG815Now

December 19

Sign

> "This will be a sign for you: You will find a baby wrapped in strips of cloth and lying in a manger"
>
> — Luke 2:12

A STRANGE SIGN.

A baby in a manger.

What does it mean?

Jesus came because we made such a mess of things. God said, "I will not leave you alone. I will not let you destroy yourself, each other, and the world I made." After we had trashed everything, God said, "I'm coming down there so you'll know once and for all how much I love you." We didn't pay any attention; it didn't even make sense to us. How could God visit us? But he did—and he came to the world in a most unlikely way. He entered a virgin's womb and came out as a baby, born in Bethlehem, a baby named Jesus, born to save us from our sins.

When he grew up, we killed him. Murdered him. Hung him on a cross. That's the thanks we gave to God for visiting us. But we were wrong about everything. After we killed him, he came back from the dead—proving he was right all along, and we were really wrong—dead wrong about everything—and still God loved us and came from heaven to earth on the greatest rescue mission in history.

He came because we blew it so badly.

He came and we killed him.

He died and became our Savior.

Only God could have done something like that. What a story! What a Christ! C.S. Lewis said, "The son of God became a man to enable men to become the sons of God." God has done it all. God wrapped up his Son in swaddling clothes and said to the whole world, "This is my Christmas gift to you."

That's the sign!

We mess things up, and God sends a baby in a manger.

This is the central truth of Christianity. *God has entered human history to provide for our salvation.* What we could not do, he did for us through his Son. Everything else flows from this truth. If he had not been born, he could not have died for our sins. And he would not have risen from the dead. He had to become like us to save us. There was no other way.

Christmas matters because truth matters. God did not leave us alone, but in our misery, he came to visit us one dark night in Bethlehem 2,000 years ago.

Christmas is all about who we are, and who God is, and how far he will go for us.

The sign of his love is a baby wrapped in rags lying in a manger.

Lord Jesus, we are like sheep, always going astray. We need you more than we know! Come, Lord, we need you right now. Amen.

Musical Bonus
Sometimes our doubts may overwhelm us. That's when we go back to what we know to be true. Let's listen as Anne Wilson sings *I Still Believe in Christmas.*
https://youtu.be/kKkFyaRpfUo

December 20

Terrified

"Then an angel of the Lord stood before them, and the glory of the Lord shone around them, and they were terrified"

— Luke 2:9

TRANSLATORS HANDLE that last word in various ways:
"Terrified."
"Very frightened."
"Sore afraid."
I like that last one the best because it's both archaic and descriptive. Though we never use the phrase "sore afraid," we know exactly what it means.

It's the natural reaction when God suddenly enters our world. One moment you and the other shepherds are chatting out in the fields while the sheep sleep peacefully. It's a beautiful night in Judea, the sky is filled with stars, and you are glad to be there.

Suddenly an angel shows up and scares you to death. If an angel of the Lord stood before me in the middle of the night, I would be "sore afraid" too.

This seems to happen whenever an angel shows up for the first time:

The angel said to Mary, "Fear not" (Luke 1:30).
The angel said to Joseph, "Fear not" (Matthew 1:20).
The angel said to the shepherds, "Fear not" (Luke 2:10).

Sometimes we need a "divine disruption" so that God can speak clearly to us. When Christ came to this sad world, God sent the angels to say, "Pay attention. Something big is happening here!"

If our greatest need had been education, God would have sent a teacher.

If our greatest need had been money, God would have sent a banker. If our greatest need had been advice, God would have sent a counselor.

But since our greatest need was forgiveness, God sent a Savior. His name is Jesus. He is Christ the Lord, the Son of God who came from heaven to earth.

Are you overcome with worry? Weighed down with fear? Are you "sore afraid" about your future? God's answer to your fear is not a theory or a doctrine. God's answer is not a seminar or a book to read. *God wrapped his answer in a baby named Jesus.* He alone is the Lord from heaven. He alone can save us. All that God has for you and me is wrapped up in his Son. No matter what difficulties we face or the decisions we must make, in the end God leads us back to that simple one-word answer: "Jesus."

In an interview with David Frost on PBS, Billy Graham said he hoped the last word he uttered before dying was simply this: "Jesus." We can't do any better than that.

Heavenly Father, may faith rise to banish our fear because if God be for us, who can be against us? Amen.

Musical Bonus
Christmas is only five days away. Let's get in the mood by listening to *Hark! The Herald Angels Sing* by Diamond Rio.
https://youtu.be/GhNFocFTKz0

December 21

Until

"After listening to the king, they went on their way. And behold, the star that they had seen when it rose went before them until it came to rest over the place where the child was"

— Matthew 2:9

WHAT EXACTLY WAS the "star" the Wise Men saw in the east?

Frankly, we don't know. The Greek word is a very general one that could refer to any bright object in the sky. It might mean a star or a planet or a meteor or even a comet. It could refer to some unusual conjunction of the planets that produced an extremely bright object in the skies. Or perhaps the "star" was a special heavenly light prepared by God to guide the Magi.

Somehow they knew it was "his" star, which is why they were overjoyed when they saw it (Matthew 2:10). It led them to the home where Mary and Joseph were taking care of the baby. That doesn't sound like a comet or a meteor to me. It sounds more like a special light from God sent to direct the Magi to Jesus.

They followed it until it came to rest over the place where the child was. *The word "until" means the guidance was very precise.* The star was a kind of divine GPS that led them from Persia in the east to Jerusalem in the west and from Jerusalem to Bethlehem and then to the precise house where Jesus was staying with Mary and Joseph.

The star seems to have appeared in the east and then disappeared. That explains why they were overjoyed when they saw the star as they traveled from Jerusalem to Bethlehem (Matthew 2:10). The reappearance of the star meant they were on the right track.

Soon they would meet the infant "King of the Jews."

God always gives us enough guidance to do his will. Did they know the star would reappear on the road to Bethlehem? No, but it happened in the ordinary course of events. As they followed the light they were given, God sent the star to lead them to the exact location of the child.

God arranged their journey from Persia to Bethlehem so that they would meet Jesus and worship him.

It is no different for us.

Let us lay aside our cares and follow the Wise Men on their journey to Bethlehem. A baby lies there who is the Light of the World. The King in the cradle. Immanuel. God with us. The Lamb of God who takes away the sin of the world. Jesus, Savior, Wonderful Counselor, Mighty God, Everlasting Father, Prince of Peace.

Lord Jesus, may we be like the Wise Men who were guided to you by a star. Give us wisdom to seek you and light to find you. Amen.

Musical Bonus
In a world filled with doubt and skepticism, Gordon Mote reminds us that *The Star Still Shines.*
https://youtu.be/ez0uCqQw7Rg

December 22

Virgin

"The virgin will conceive and bear a son, and they will call his name Immanuel"

— Matthew 1:23

Do you believe in the Virgin Birth?

What difference does it make?

Let's start with the first question. For almost 2000 years Christians have repeated this phrase from the Apostles Creed: "Conceived of the Holy Spirit, born of the Virgin Mary." Although Christians have disagreed on almost everything, here is a truth unanimously affirmed by all branches of the Christian church.

We believe Jesus was born of a virgin.

That forces us to confront what we believe about Jesus Christ. Who is he? Where did he come from? *At issue is the supernatural character of our Lord.* Is he truly the Son of God from heaven? If you answer yes, you'll have no problem with the virgin birth. If you answer no, you'll have no reason to believe it.

Christians make a claim for Jesus that cannot be made for any other person: *His life did not begin with his birth or with his conception.* Unlike every other human whose beginning can be traced to a specific moment in time, the true life of Jesus Christ had no beginning. Because he is eternal, he existed forever with God the Father and God the Holy Spirit. This is an utterly supernatural claim that could not be made about anyone else.

Here is another way to state the same truth. For Christ to be our Savior, three conditions must be met:

1. *He must be a man.* An angel could not die for our sins. He must share our humanity.
2. *He must be an infinite man.* A mere mortal could not bear the infinite price that must be paid for our sins.

45

3. *He must be an innocent man.* A sinner could not die for the sins of others.

Our Lord fulfills all three conditions.

Because he is born of Mary, he is fully human.

Because he is conceived by the Holy Spirit, he is fully God.

Because he is born holy, he is sinless in thought, word, and deed.

Thus, he is fully qualified to be our Savior.

The angel told Joseph to name him Jesus *"for he will save his people from their sins"* (Matthew 1:21). *That connects his birth with his saving work on the cross.* The virgin birth matters because it tells us who Jesus is and lays the foundation for the great work he will accomplish on the cross.

He had to be born this way to die the way he died.

We are not saved by the virgin birth, but without it we are not saved at all.

Almighty God, may we not stumble in unbelief but believe in your Son, our Savior, born of a virgin, who died for our salvation, rose from the dead, ascended into heaven, and is our coming king. Amen.

Musical Bonus

Here's a new version of a familiar carol. Let's listen to *The First Noel* by Point of Grace.
https://youtu.be/yfnxxUnc1S0

December 23

Wonder

"All who heard it wondered at what the shepherds told them"

— Luke 2:18

SOME TRANSLATIONS USE wondered.

Others say amazed.

Others use the word marveled.

The story itself sounds incredible, especially the part about hearing the angels in the middle of the night, not to mention finding the Son of God in a feeding trough. It's even more surprising that God chose lowly shepherds as the first evangelists.

Amazement comes in two varieties. The first has to do with temporary fascination over an unusual turn of events. It's what happens when a five-touchdown underdog manages to win a football game. Terrible teams occasionally get lucky and beat much better teams. It's unusual but not miraculous.

The second kind of amazement we could call "Holy Wonder." It's awe that comes from seeing God at work in the world. Go all the way back to Genesis and you discover God created the entire universe out of nothing. He spoke and the stars flew into place. He spoke and the earth took up its orbit. He spoke and the squirrels began to scamper through the forest.

God speaks and it happens. He takes a lump of dirt and makes a man. Then he takes a rib and makes a woman. When we read Genesis 1-2, we encounter something truly wonderful, that is, full of wonders on every hand.

The wonders continue to the very end of the Bible. Revelation 19 tells us that when Christ returns, he will have written on his robe and on his thigh, *"King of Kings and Lord of Lords"* (Revelation 19:16). When Christ returns, he will establish his kingdom on the earth, and all earthly kings will bow before him.

Christmas is indeed a cause for holy wonder. How can it be that God should become a man? How can a King be born in a feeding trough? How could the world ignore his coming? And what sort of God comes into the world like this?

We ought to be amazed at Christmastime. If we go through this season without ever pausing to think about the wonder of it all, then we have missed the reason we celebrate Christmas in the first place.

Lord Jesus, we long to be transformed by the wonder of your coming. Free us from our addiction to the mundane. Give us the faith of a child so that we can laugh with joy once again. Amen.

Musical Bonus
During the Civil War, Henry Wadsworth Longfellow penned a poem that expresses the hope for "peace on earth, goodwill to men." Let's listen as Sleeping at Last sings *I Heard the Bells.*
https://youtu.be/agB5Nh1rT2k

"For unto you is born this day in the city of David a
Savior, who is Christ the Lord"

— Luke 2:11

There aren't many words that start with X.

I checked the dictionary, found a few, and couldn't pronounce
most of them because they are words we rarely use.

Then it hit me.

The letter X is an ancient symbol for Christ because it stands for
the first letter in the Greek word for Christ:

Χρίστος (pronounced "chris-tos").

R. C. Sproul explains it this way:

> Christos is the New Testament Greek for Christ. The first letter
> of the Greek word Christos is transliterated into our alphabet
> as an X. That X has come through church history to be a
> shorthand symbol for the name of Christ.

Luke 2:11 uses three words to describe him: *Savior … Christ …
Lord.* Each word is vitally important. *Savior* is an Old Testament word
that means "one who delivers his people." *Christ* is the Greek version of
the Hebrew word Messiah, which means "the anointed One." *Lord* is a
term for Deity. It's a synonym for God.

I received a letter from a prisoner in Wisconsin who had read *An
Anchor for the Soul.* The oldest of five children, he came from a single-
parent family. He joined a gang and dropped out of school in the ninth
grade. At the age of 17, he was arrested, tried, and convicted of first-
degree murder. Sentenced to life in prison, he had been behind bars for
19 years when he wrote me. This is his comment: "Dr. Pritchard, many
had given up on me, but God never did! I was told that I would never

amount to anything but God says otherwise. I was told that I would find death in prison but instead I found eternal life."

How does he feel about his 19 years behind bars?

I have been so overwhelmed by the grace and mercy of Christ—I've been given a wonderful peace that surpasses all understanding. I am absolutely convinced that had I not come to prison, my life would have been completely devastated beyond repair. It's now been 19 years of incarceration and these years have been the most refreshing and enlightening years of my life—I am truly blessed beyond words.

Only the grace of God can enable a man to talk like that. He even wants to write a book about his life story called Saved by the Cell. That's why Christ came—to be a Savior for everyone who will turn to him.

He is the Savior, he is the Lord, and he is the Christ—the one sent from God. *This is the heart of Christmas.* God loved us enough to send his only begotten Son.

X stands for Christ who is our Savior and Lord. And that's what Christmas is all about.

We call you Lord because that is what you are. We call you Savior because you came to save us from our sins. We call you Christ because all God's promises are fulfilled in you. Glory to you, Lord Jesus Christ, now and forever! Amen.

Musical Bonus
Happy Christmas Eve! To celebrate this wonderful day, let's listen as Anna Hawkins sings *O Holy Night*.
https://youtu.be/G7uSSXqwDcI

December 25

You

"For unto you is born this day in the city of David a Savior, who is Christ the Lord"

— Luke 2:11

"Unto you."

Pause for a moment and consider who was speaking and who was being addressed. When the shepherds heard these words from the angel, they must have been flabbergasted. Shepherds were near the bottom of the social order of ancient Israel. They were often poor and uneducated, and some were quite young. *Not very many people would put "shepherd" on their Career Preference Form.* There were many easier ways to make a living in ancient Israel. So when the angel says, "To you is born," he's really saying, "Christ came for lowly shepherds." But what about those theologians in Jerusalem who knew but didn't care? He came for them too, but they missed it altogether.

When Christ came, his birth was first announced to the outcasts of society. *They were the first ones to hear the good news of Christmas.* There is a great lesson in this for all of us. Our Lord came for the forgotten people of the earth, and most of the time they are the ones who receive him with the greatest joy. Rich people often have no time for Christ, but the poor welcome him as an honored guest.

A man traveled a great distance for an interview with a distinguished scholar. He was ushered into the man's study, where he said, "Doctor, I notice that the walls of your study are lined with books from the ceiling to the floor. No doubt you have read them all. I know you have written many yourself. You have traveled extensively, and doubtless you've had the privilege of conversing with some of the world's wisest men. I've come a long way to ask you just one question. Tell me, of all you've learned, what is the one thing most worth knowing?" Putting his hand on his guest's shoulder, the scholar replied with emotion in his voice,

51

"My dear sir, of all the things I have learned, only two are really worth knowing. The first is, I am a great sinner, and the second is, Jesus Christ is a great Savior!"

If you know those two things, you know the best news in the whole world, that a Savior has been born for you who is Christ the Lord.

Two thousand years ago God sent a gift wrapped in swaddling clothes and lying in a manger.

Jesus is God's gift to you.

Merry Christmas!

The happy day is here at last.

Joy to the world, the Lord is come!

Lord of all, we come before you, celebrating this happy day when Eternity entered time, and the Infinite became finite. You who were rich became poor that we through your poverty might be rich. Give us ears to hear the glad tidings and voices to sing with exuberant praise that at long last our Redeemer has come! Amen.

Musical Bonus

Sometimes we need to remember that Christmas is for our children. Let's listen as the Salzburg Children's Choir sings *Silent Night*. https://youtu.be/Ti8kLr2NzTI

December 26

Zion

"O Zion, you who bring good tidings … Say to the
cities of Judah, 'Behold your God!'"

— Isaiah 40:9 NKJV

WHEN HANDEL COMPOSED his famous oratorio The Messiah, he
included a piece based on this verse ("Oh thou that tellest good tidings
to Zion") combined with Isaiah 60:1, "Arise, shine, for your light has
come." In the order of songs, it comes right after the prediction of the
virgin birth in Isaiah 7:14, "Behold, a virgin shall conceive." It was
Handel's way of saying, "This is how we should respond to Christ's
birth."

Go and tell.

Share the good news.

Arise and let your light shine.

*These are good words for today because Christmas eventually ends
for all of us.* Soon enough we will take down the tree, pack away the
ornaments, and either use our gifts or take them back to the store to
be exchanged. In a few days the children go back to school, and life
returns to normal.

But will we be changed by Christmas?

People sometimes wish they could keep the Christmas spirit all
year long. They speak of it as if the "magic" of these days comes only
once a year. *But it depends on what "magic" you are talking about.* If you
mean the tree and the gifts and the mistletoe and the chestnuts roasting
on an open fire, that indeed comes only once a year. But the greater
truth of Christmas ought to warm our hearts long after the holiday has
ended.

Would you like Christmas to last all year long? It can if you will
take Isaiah's words to heart. So go back to where you came from.

Back to your office.

Back to your classroom.

Back to your factory.

Back to your neighborhood.

Back to your job.

Back to your family duties.

Go back to the humdrum of daily routine. *But do not go back unchanged.* Arise and let your light shine. When the shepherds saw Jesus, they couldn't stop talking about it. Christmas didn't change their circumstances, but it changed them deeply and profoundly. Yes, they still had to deal with cranky sheep and sometimes they had to step in sheep manure, but that hardly mattered now.

They had seen the Christ child.

Have you seen Jesus this year at Christmastime? If you have, then go back to what you were doing before and take the memory of Christmas with you. *Start where you are, and God will be with you.*

With that thought, our Advent Alphabet comes to an end. But if you go and tell the good news of Jesus, you will have Christmas all year long.

Grant to us, O Lord, the wonder of Mary, the obedience of Joseph, the joy of the angels, the eagerness of the shepherds, the determination of the Magi, and the peace of the Christ child. Amen.

Musical Bonus

We wrap up our journey through the Advent Alphabet with a beloved American spiritual. Here's a hand-clapping, toe-tapping arrangement of *Go Tell It On the Mountain* by MercyMe.
https://youtu.be/5xTTBI1zxL4

We hope you have enjoyed this journey through the Advent season!

Would you consider donating so we can continue to offer the electronic version of this book and thousands of other resources free to people around the world through our website?

Thank you, and God bless you!

Donate to Keep Believing Ministries
https://www.keepbelieving.com/donate/

Made in the USA
Monee, IL
25 October 2022

16483518R10037